Food Chains

Alvin Silverstein, Virginia Silverstein,
and Laura Silverstein Nunn

 Twenty-First Century Books
Minneapolis

Twenty-First Century Books
A division of Lerner Publishing Group, Inc.
241 First Avenue North
Minneapolis, Minnesota 55401 U.S.A.

Website address: www.lernerbooks.com

Library of Congress Cataloging-in-Publication Data

Silverstein, Alvin
    Food Chains / Alvin Silverstein, Virginia Silverstein, Laura Silverstein Nunn.
    — Rev. ed.
        p.   cm. — (Science concepts)
    Includes bibliographical references and index.
    ISBN-13: 978–0–8225–6797–4 (lib. bdg. : alk. paper)
    1. Food chains (Ecology)—Juvenile literature. [1. Food chains (Ecology)
2. Ecology.] I. Silverstein. Virginia B. II. Nunn, Laura Silverstein. III. Title.
IV. Series: Silverstein, Alvin. Science concepts.
QH541.S534 2008
577'.16—dc22   2007003186

Manufactured in the United States of America
1 2 3 4 5 6 — DP — 13 12 11 10 09 08

Contents

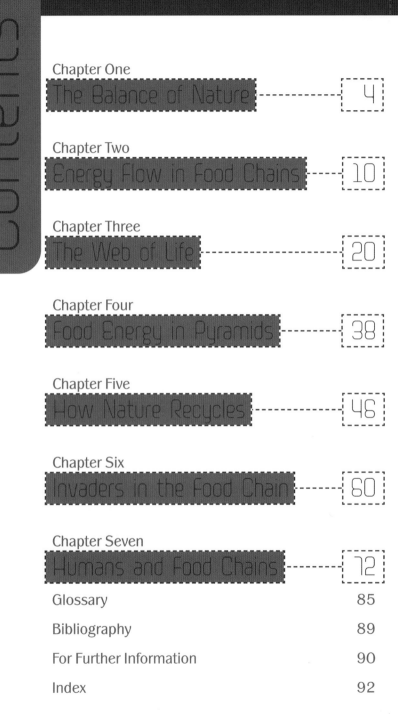

Chapter One
The Balance of Nature ---------- 4

Chapter Two
Energy Flow in Food Chains ----- 10

Chapter Three
The Web of Life ---------------- 20

Chapter Four
Food Energy in Pyramids -------- 38

Chapter Five
How Nature Recycles ------------ 46

Chapter Six
Invaders in the Food Chain ----- 60

Chapter Seven
Humans and Food Chains --------- 72

Glossary   85

Bibliography   89

For Further Information   90

Index   92

During the early 1900s, about four thousand mule deer could be found munching on the leaves, weeds, grass, clover, and mushrooms in the Kaibab National Forest in Arizona, north of the Grand Canyon. The deer population was stable until 1907, when hunters in the area decided to increase the numbers of deer by eliminating their natural predators, such as mountain lions, coyotes, and wolves.

The hunters could not have predicted the impact they would have on the environment. By 1924 the deer population increased to an astounding one hundred thousand. These plant-eating animals stripped the land of all its green plant life. They even ate the bark off trees. Their food became scarce, and many starved to death. Deer that wandered into other areas to forage often did not survive. Weakened deer gave birth to stillborn and defective fawns. In 1939 the mule deer population had dramatically declined to about ten thousand.

The Kaibab National Forest is presently a national game preserve, and the animals in the area

Mule deer like this one are now protected by wildlife officials at the Kaibab National Forest in Arizona.

are protected by wildlife officials. The Forest Service has devised a management plan that regulates the size of the mule deer population. The excess deer are killed either by predators or by hunters until there is a balance between the number of deer and the amount of food the land can produce.

A Food Connection

All living organisms within an environment are connected through a common link—food. For example, plants need sun, rain, and nutrients from the soil so they can grow. Some animals in the area eat the plants for food. Other animals eat smaller or weaker animals for food. Some animals feed on both plants and animals. Scientists are able to keep track of such relationships by listing the plant and animal species in food chains. Basically, a

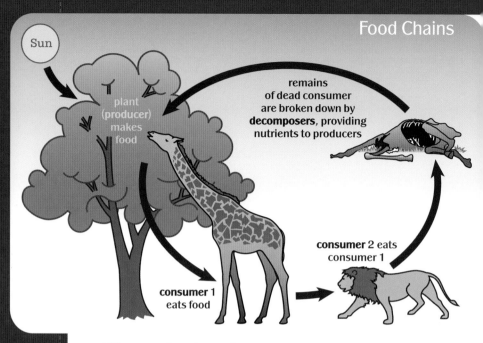

Who eats whom in the food chain? Plants make their own food. In turn, they are food for animals, which may later be eaten by other animals. When living things die, they are food for decomposers, which break down their bodies into simple materials that plants can use to make food.

food chain indicates "who eats whom."

Animals and plants that live together in the same area, such as the Kaibab National Forest, belong to a biological community. All living organisms in a biological community, including plants and animals, depend on other living and nonliving things in some way. The science that deals with the interdependent relationships between living organisms and their habitat is called ecology. The German zoologist Ernst Haeckel coined the term *ecology* in 1869 from two Greek roots: *oikos*, meaning "household," and *ology*,

The ecosystem in the Canadian Rockies has everything from trees and grasses to Canadian geese (pictured) *and elk.*

meaning "study of." He recognized that organisms do not live alone. Instead, they are part of a "household," a community that includes various organisms together with their physical surroundings. A community in which organisms live and interact with one another and their environment is called an ecosystem. Ecosystems exist in all the varied places on our planet, from forests, plains, and deserts to lakes, streams, and oceans.

Finding a Niche in Society

Every organism in a community has a niche, a specific role within a community. A niche can be described as a job, or a way of living. There are three types of niches: producers, consumers, and decomposers. Producers include almost all

Animals in a food chain are all linked as one organism feeds on another, such as a fox that feeds on a rabbit.

plants. Their role is to provide food for the other organisms in the community. Consumers eat other organisms in the community. Their role is to feed on producers or other consumers or both. For instance, rabbits are consumers because they eat grass and other plants (producers). But foxes are also consumers because they eat rabbits (which are consumers). As one organism feeds on another, which feeds on still another, they are linked into a food chain. Any food chain ends eventually with decomposers, which include fungi and bacteria. Their role is to get rid of the dead organisms in the community.

Each link in a food chain must be strong enough

Decomposers, such as these mushrooms, break down animal and plant matter into compounds that enrich the soil. This process also returns carbon dioxide into the air, where green plants use it to make food.

to ensure the survival of all the organisms involved. When one link is weakened or broken, as happened when most of the mule-deer predators at Kaibab were wiped out, the rest of the food chain is affected either directly or indirectly. A single change in the environment can affect the organisms living in it and thus upset the balance of nature.

chapter two

Energy Flow in Food Chains

What do the sun, a field of grass, a rabbit, and a fox have in common? They are all connected in a food chain. The sun shines on a field of grass and gives it energy to grow. A rabbit comes hopping along, stops to nibble on the grass, and gets energy from the meal. Hiding behind a bush, a fox comes out and tries to catch the rabbit. The rabbit sees the fox and tries to escape. The fox chases the rabbit. The chase ends when the fox catches the rabbit, and it becomes food for the fox, which in turn gets energy from this meal. This food chain illustrates the transfer of energy from one organism to another.

Food Makers

All living things need energy in order to live. They use energy to breathe, hunt, and reproduce. Almost all the energy that living things on Earth use comes originally from the sun. But most creatures cannot use sunlight directly. Green plants—whether an oak tree or a dandelion—as well as the algae in a pond or ocean and certain bacteria are the only living organisms that can use sunlight energy to make their own food. They do this through a process called photosynthesis.

The sun provides the energy for plants to make their own food through photo-synthesis.

Photosynthesis, as its name suggests, uses sunlight energy (the *photo-* part of the word) to put simple chemicals together to form more complex ones (a *synthesis*). Plants need water, carbon dioxide, and nitrogen compounds from the atmosphere for photosynthesis. Using the energy of sunlight, they turn these raw materials into sugars, starches, and other carbohydrates. Green plants get their color from chlorophyll. This green pigment absorbs sunlight energy to power the chemical reactions of photosynthesis. Part of the sunlight energy is converted to chemical energy, which is stored in the plant's tissues. Photosynthesis takes place both in the water and on land. The need for sunlight is the reason why many water plants live in shallow waters rather than in the deep sea.

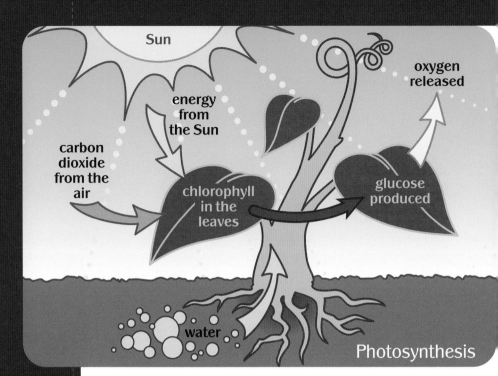

Photosynthesis

Photosynthesis is the process by which green plants make their food. The process begins when sunlight interacts with the chlorophyll in the plant's leaves and light energy is stored as chemical energy in the chloroplasts. Water and carbon dioxide also enter the leaf. The carbon dioxide combines with water, using the energy stored in the chloroplasts, to produce sugar. The sugar is then transported to other parts of the plant and either stored, used right away for energy, or used to make other food substances.

Members of a Food Chain

Producers are the first link in food chains. Plants are producers because they can make their own food through photosynthesis. These photosynthetic organisms are also called autotrophs, from the Greek words for "self-feeders."

Making Food without Photosynthesis

Just 500 miles (800 km) southwest of Acapulco, Mexico, and about 1.5 miles (2.5 km) beneath the surface of the Pacific Ocean, a team of researchers in 1991 discovered an interesting biological community where an alternative energy source is used by living things. The sun is necessary for photosynthesis. But sunlight cannot reach the deep sea bottom. However, in this environment, life can grow because there are underwater volcanic fissures, called hydrothermal vents. These vents are like miniature underwater volcanoes. When they "erupt," they kill everything in sight and heat the waters to 400°F (200°C).

Heat is a form of energy. Bacteria that live at the bottom near the vents get heat from the depths of Earth. They use its energy and the chemical energy of sulfur compounds in the water to make food. This kind of food production is called chemosynthesis. The bacteria continue to grow and flourish. Soon consumers such as crabs and other crustaceans come to feed on the bacteria. Other sea animals, such as tube worms and mussels, feed on the bacteria as well. Within only a year, in this environment without sunlight, the number of species living around the vents can double.

Mad Cow Consumer

Cows are very important animals in society. Many people use them as a source of food. What cows eat can have a serious effect in the food chain. Normally, cows are primary consumers because they feed on grasses and grains. But livestock may be given feed that contains animal parts, making them secondary consumers.

In June 1997, the U.S. government banned this practice of adding animal parts to cattle feed because of the deadly mad cow disease. This disease had sickened and killed some people in Great Britain who had eaten contaminated beef. The disease was spread by a microorganism in the flesh of infected animals. By supplementing the cows' feed with animal parts, British farmers had added a new, unnatural link in the food chain and thus exposed their cows to infection. New rules in the United States protect our cattle—and the people who eat their meat—by limiting them to a plant diet.

Autotrophs are the basis of all food chains because they produce food not only for themselves but for all other organisms, either directly or indirectly. For instance, when a rabbit eats grass, it gets the food energy stored in the plants directly. But when a fox eats the rabbit, the fox gets the plant food energy indirectly through the rabbit. And the food energy continues to be passed on up the food chain.

The next links in food chains are consumers, organisms that cannot make their own food and must eat other organisms to live. They are known as heterotrophs, from the Greek words for "other feeders." There are three types of these consumers: herbivores, carnivores, and omnivores. Herbivores, such as grasshoppers, rabbits, deer, and cows, are animals that eat mostly plants. Carnivores, such as foxes and mountain lions, are animals that eat other animals. Carnivores play an important role in food chains because they help to regulate the number of herbivores and thus maintain the balance of nature. Omnivores, such as raccoons and bears, are animals that eat both plants and animals. Most humans are also omnivores. We may have a meal that includes a salad and a steak (a producer and a consumer).

Decomposers and scavengers form a special group of heterotrophs. Decomposers are organisms, such as fungi and bacteria, that get food by breaking down the remains of dead plants and animals into nutrients. They also break down the waste materials of living organisms. This is an important job because the nutrients enter the soil and help new plants to grow. Scavengers, such as vultures, also feed on the bodies of dead animals. Decomposers and scavengers can be found at every level of the food chain. They get food

Vultures can quickly remove the flesh from a dead animal. Vultures are scavengers. Along with decomposers, they are found at every level of the food chain.

for themselves and allow materials to be reused by the organisms in the food chains.

Keeping Track of Food Energy

A food chain is like a ladder, with animals at each step. The animals at higher levels eat the animals below them. Each step is known as a trophic level (from the Greek word for "food"). Trophic levels track the transfer of food energy and nourishment among the organisms in an ecosystem. Following a single food chain, we can see how energy moves from one trophic level to the next. For example, a plant that changes energy from the sun into chemical energy during photosynthesis may use part of this energy to form flowers that contain nectar and pollen. A moth that drinks the flowers' sweet nectar may be snapped up by a frog. Later, the frog may be swallowed by a snake, which in turn becomes a meal for a swooping hawk.

The first trophic level begins with the primary producer (the flowering plant). The primary producer provides food for the first-level, or primary, consumer (the moth), typically an herbivore. The primary consumer is eaten by the second-level, or secondary, consumer (the frog), which may be a carnivore or omnivore. The secondary consumer is eaten by the third-level, or tertiary, consumer (the snake), which may also be a carnivore or omnivore. Sometimes there may be a fourth-level, or quaternary, consumer (hawk). Some consumers can change

Life in a Compost Heap

A compost heap is the perfect environment for decomposers and scavengers. People can efficiently recycle plant wastes by gathering leaves, grass clippings, potato peelings, and other vegetation and putting the material in a compost pile. An effective compost heap consists of layers of organic wastes alternating with thin layers of soil. The mixture is watered to speed up the process. Once the decomposers and scavengers go to work, the bacteria multiply and the organic wastes decay at amazing speeds. The rotting mixture inside a compost heap can reach very high temperatures—up to 130°F (54°C). When the compost is ready, people may use it as a fertilizer to make their gardens more productive or as a mulch around their plants.

Trophic Levels in a Food Chain

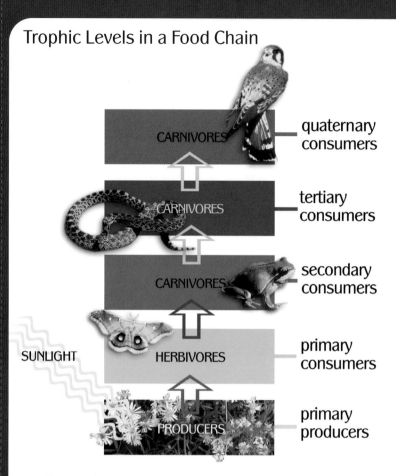

CARNIVORES — quaternary consumers

CARNIVORES — tertiary consumers

CARNIVORES — secondary consumers

SUNLIGHT HERBIVORES — primary consumers

PRODUCERS — primary producers

Food chains can be divided into a series of trophic levels, like the steps on a ladder. Each kind of organism in the chain is eaten by those in the level above it.

levels. For instance, if the hawk eats a mouse that ate seeds, it is a secondary consumer. But the hawk is a tertiary consumer if it eats a mouse that ate insects. When the highest-level consumer in the food chain dies, decomposers and scavengers get rid of it as well as the remains of the other dead organisms at each trophic level.

Nature's Pooper-Scooper

Decomposers have a little helper when it comes to cleaning up the environment. In the West African savannas, a member of the scarab family known as the dung beetle is nature's pooper-scooper. These beetles bury the dung of animals and store it to feed themselves and their families. They work very fast, sometimes burying it within hours. Within a year, hard-working beetles living on 1 acre (0.4 hectare) can bury about half a ton (0.5 metric ton) of dung.

Dung beetles are important in the environment. Without their help, the ground would be covered with dung. Minerals and other nutrients in the dung are recycled in the process, providing a natural fertilizer that helps plants to grow.

chapter three

The Web of Life

What would it be like if animals in the wild ate the same thing day after day? Not only would their life lack variety, but it would also be precarious. What would happen, for example, if lions could eat only zebras? If a natural disaster, such as a raging fire, wiped out the entire zebra population in an area, the lions that lived there would lose their only food source. Soon they, too, would die out.

Actually, however, lions will eat many kinds of animals—not only zebras but also antelope, buffalo, warthogs, turtles, and guinea fowl, depending on what prey is available. Their prey, in turn, can feed on a variety of plant life, depending on what is plentiful. Each kind of plant may provide food for a variety of animals. In most ecosystems, there are thus many food chains that are linked to form a complex food web. The diversity of these food webs increases the chances of each species' survival.

The food web, or the "web of life," describes how animals, plants, and other organisms are connected in an ecosystem—how they feed on one another.

Lions' prey consists mainly of large mammals, such as antelopes, gazelles, warthogs, wildebeest, buffalo and zebras, but smaller animals such as hares and birds are also taken occasionally. Their diet consists of only about twenty different species, but this diversity helps increase a species chances for survival and is an example of a complex food web. A food web is many food chains linked.

Most animals eat a variety of foods every day. A few animals, however, eat the same food day after day. The koalas of Australia, for instance, can often be found sitting in eucalyptus trees. They eat mostly the leaves and young shoots of these trees. Koalas in the wild do not drink water—they get their liquids from the eucalyptus leaves. Thus, they are completely dependent on the trees. If a disaster destroyed the eucalyptus trees, many koalas would not survive.

The giant panda of central China is already in serious danger for a similar reason. The pandas live in dense bamboo forests, and bamboo shoots and roots make up about 95 percent of their diet. (They also eat flowers, fish, and small rodents.) The panda can get only about 17 percent of the nutrients out of its high-fiber diet. It eats 20 to 40 pounds (9 to 18 kilogram) of bamboo each day and spends up to fourteen hours a day feeding. But commercial development is shrinking the bamboo forests, threatening both the panda's home and its food supply.

The Food Web

Most animals can eat many kinds of food and thus are included in a number of different food chains. These separate chains form a complicated food web, linking all the organisms of the community.

Biodiversity—a variety of species at each trophic level—is essential for the health of a biological community. The more varied an animal's diet, the better chance it has of surviving. A variety of animals eating a particular kind of plant may help to keep it from overgrowing and choking out other plant species. Animals also help plants to reproduce by pollinating their flowers and distributing their seeds.

In the modern world, however, human activities have been decreasing biodiversity. People kill animals and plants they regard as pests, but they can also wipe out species unintentionally. When people clear

Who's More Important?

Who's more important in a biological community—a towering elephant or a tiny fruit bat? The answer: They are equally important. In the rain forest, elephants eat a lot of plants—as much as 500 pounds (225 kg) a day each! This lets sunlight through, helping more plants grow for other animals to eat. Elephants also use their tusks to dig out hard-to-find watering holes, which is necessary for many animals during the dry season.

Fruit bats not only eat fruit, they also plant it. With their tough outer coating, many seeds pass through a bat's digestive system unharmed and fall to the ground with its droppings. One bat can drop as many as sixty thousand seeds in a single night. In this way, bats actually help to regrow the rain forest after it has been cut down. It is not an animal's size that is important, but what it does in the environment.

forests to make farms or build roads and cities, wild creatures lose their food and living space. Pollution from human industries has also damaged natural communities. When species die out, there are far-reaching effects on the other members of their ecosystems. A food web can be compared to a spider web: If a couple of strands are broken, a spider web can still keep its shape. But if too many strands break, the whole web is in danger of collapsing.

The Key to Survival

Food webs include both strong and weak relationships among species. Some species, called keystone species, have a significant effect on their communities. In fact, other members in

A mountain lion plays an important part in maintaining the balance among all the species that live in its biological community.

the community depend on this species for survival. In a building, a keystone is the wedge-shaped piece at the crown of an arch that locks the other pieces in place. Without that key piece, everything surrounding it will fall. A mountain lion is a keystone species because it keeps a balance among all living things in its food web. When mountain lions were hunted at the Kaibab National Forest, a disastrous chain reaction was started. Once the mountain lions disappeared from the community, the mule deer multiplied greatly and ate all the available plant material. Soon there was not enough food for everyone, and many animals starved to death.

A keystone species can help to maintain diversity within a biological community in two ways. It may control the population of a species that might otherwise multiply wildly. This disrupts the balance of nature in the community, the way the mule deer multiplied when the mountain lions were gone. Or the keystone species may be a vital resource for a wide range of species. Thus, the keystone species helps to preserve the environment and everything in it, big or small—deer, rabbits, butterflies, plants, and even mosquitoes.

In the ocean, the shark is a keystone species. The shark has a bad reputation as a murderous beast. But the shark, like the mountain lion, is essential for the survival of all living things in its community. The shark eats a lot of fish and other sea animals. It also helps to keep the ocean waters clean by eating dead or sick fish.

Sharks are a keystone species that keep ocean waters clean and keep the fish population in check.

If sharks disappeared from the underwater world, the waters would become dirty and overpopulated with fish. The larger fish would eat all the tiny fish and other water animals that feed on the algae. Then algae would grow so much that the waters would become thick with slime.

A keystone species, such as the mountain lion or the shark, may also be considered an umbrella species. If an umbrella species is protected, then many other animals are protected at the same time. However, not all umbrella species are keystone species. A keystone species is essential to its environment and all the animals that live in it. Without it, the ecosystem would fall apart. An umbrella species is also important, but its removal does not necessarily cause a serious breakdown in the community. For instance, the spotted owl is an umbrella species in the forests of the northwestern United States.

The spotted owl is an endangered species, and its habitats in the Pacific Northwest are protected. Other species living in the same habitats also benefit from the protection.

Spotted owls need a lot of space to live and hunt. If enough habitat is preserved for the spotted owl, then the other animals that live in the area are automatically protected at the same time.

Nature's Defenses

All biological communities include predators and prey. Predators are animals that hunt and kill other animals for food. (In trophic terms, they are secondary, or higher-level, consumers.) Prey are animals that are killed by other animals for food. (They are usually primary consumers but may also include some secondary consumers, such as mice or frogs that eat insects and are in turn eaten by other animals.) Predator and prey interactions are nature's way of keeping a healthy balance in the ecosystem.

Predators cannot kill all the prey animals in their community. If they did, they would not have any food to eat in the future. Many prey animals have developed effective ways of escaping from their enemies. Some defenseless creatures are able to survive mainly because they are good at running or swimming or flying away from their enemies. For example, deer and antelope are very fast, running at up to 40 miles (64 kilometers) an hour. Many fish and birds can also move quickly. But speed alone is not enough. Some predators can run even faster than many prey. Cheetahs have been seen running as fast as 70 miles (113 km) an hour, faster than the antelope and other prey they hunt. Whales and sharks can swim 25 miles (40 km) an hour, more than twice as fast as minnows, bass, and other small fish. Eagles and falcons have been timed in flight at more than 100 miles (160 km) an hour.

An animal that survives by running away needs more than speed. Some prey animals, therefore, are not only speedy, but they can also dodge and dart about. A rabbit chased by a fox zigzags back and forth to confuse its pursuer. A minnow darts through the water, escaping the jaws of a larger fish. Some

Cheetahs can run faster than Thomson's gazelles. But the gazelles can outlast cheetahs in long chases and can make turns more speedily.

animals, such as fleas, frogs, and kangaroos, can escape their enemies by leaping into the air, reaching amazing heights.

Prey animals may use hiding places to escape from predators. A rabbit or a prairie dog will dive into an underground burrow for safety. Mice and other small rodents may use tall grasses for shelter. Some predators, such as mountain lions, however, may also use tall grasses as a hiding place. A lion will slink through the grasses unseen, ready to pounce on its prey. Before the prey knows what is happening, it is captured.

Some animals have another kind of hiding place—a built-in suit of armor. The turtle's body, for

A turtle can pull its head, legs, and tail inside its shell as a means to protect itself against predators.

example, is covered by an armorlike shell. Normally, the turtle's head, legs, and tail extend from holes in the shell. But at the first sign of danger, its head, legs, and tail suddenly disappear. All that can be seen is a tough, round shell. If a predator turns the turtle over on its back, there is a tough shell underneath as well. Predators usually give up and move on.

Other animals with a suit of armor include clams, oysters, and scallops. These shellfish, or bivalves, have two shells, which have very powerful muscles. They can snap their shells together and keep them so tightly closed that even a strong person cannot open them up. Yet some predators do manage to eat bivalves. Sea stars use suction cups on the undersides of their arms to pull a bivalve's shells open. As soon as there is a small gap between the shells, the sea star turns its stomach inside out and inserts it through the gap. It digests the bivalve right inside the shells, then pulls its stomach back inside and sucks up its meal. The oystercatcher is a bird with a long, slim

A clam's shells protect it from many predators. But a sea star can force open the shells and digest the clam's soft insides.

beak. It slips its beak in between an oyster's shells when they are open. Then, using the beak like a long pair of scissors, it quickly cuts the muscle that would snap the oyster shells shut. The sea otter also eats bivalves. This sea mammal uses a tool, such as a flat rock, to open oysters or clams. Floating on its back in

Eating Ammunition

Brightly colored frogs in the rain forests of South and Central America are hopping advertisements: "Don't eat me—I'm poisonous!" Species such as the poison dart frogs of Colombia make their own poison, batrachotoxin—one of the deadliest poisons in the world.

But other tropical frogs start out as shy, defenseless creatures. They obtain a defense by eating ants, which use poisons called alkaloids to defend themselves and capture prey. The more ants the frogs eat, the more poisonous to predators they become. Scientists found that ants make up nearly three-quarters of the diet of some frogs, which eat hundreds of ants each day. The frogs store the ant alkaloids in special glands in their skin, where they do not harm the frogs.

This crab spider has changed its color to match the black-eyed Susan flower it is sitting on. The camouflage will not only protect the spider from predators but hide the spider as it waits for unsuspecting insects that will make a tasty meal.

the water, the sea otter places the rock on its belly and cracks the bivalve shells.

Sometimes the best way for prey animals to escape from predators is to stay still. Prey that use this method typically have fur, feathers, or skin that matches their surroundings. This acts as camouflage. For instance, a green grasshopper is very hard to pick out among blades of green grass, unless it is hopping about. A crab spider sitting on a flower will change its appearance to the color of the flower. If the flower is pink, the spider will be pink too. Although this is a useful disguise against predators, it also acts as camouflage when the spider, as a predator itself, waits for an unsuspecting insect prey.

A child learns very early that a meeting with a buzzing bee can be a very painful experience. Birds that live on insects quickly learn to leave wasps and bees alone. The insects' bright-colored bodies are warning signals in the world of nature. A bee will leave a very painful memory with any predator that bothers it.

This viceroy butterfly (top) *mimics the coloring of the bad-tasting monarch butterfly* (bottom). *In areas where there aren't many monarch butterflies, viceroys resemble other kinds of bad-tasting butterflies, such as the queen butterfly.*

Other insects also use their colorful markings to warn predators. There are some orange and black butterflies that taste so bad that no bird wants to eat them. However, there are also many other orange and black butterflies that do not taste bad. Birds usually leave all of them alone because they cannot tell the difference.

Some animals defend themselves by a kind of chemical warfare. A skunk's black-and-white marking usually acts as a warning to stay away. But if the skunk is threatened, it does not need to run. It will lift its tail to the predator and spray out an extremely bad-smelling chemical. The odor lingers long after the skunk is gone. It usually takes only one encounter for an animal to learn to leave skunks alone. Some insects also use bad-smelling or stinging sprays as a chemical defense.

Nature's defenses are helpful to many animals. Even the individual animals that fall victim to predators may help to teach the predators to recognize nature's warning signals. This actually helps to keep their whole species alive.

Population Explosions

Predator/prey relationships are usually fairly successful in keeping a balance in biological communities. But sometimes certain species go through population cycles when the ecosystem is thrown out of balance. This occurs when animals reproduce so effectively that they do not have enough food or living space. Meanwhile, their population explosion affects other links in the food chains of their community, producing changes that eventually bring things back into balance.

The number of snowshoe rabbits, for example, varies over a cycle of about nine or ten years. Gradually the population builds up from year to year until enormous numbers are reached. In one area in Canada, it was estimated that the snowshoe rabbit population was once as high as 5,000 per square mile (13,000 sq. km). Then suddenly, the population dropped, without any warning, to about one-tenth of what it had been the year before. Apparently, some predators, such as lynxes, great horned owls, and goshawks, have population

A lynx reaches for its favorite food, a snowshoe rabbit. The population cycles of both animals are closely tied together. The cycles undergo changes to maintain a balance between predator and prey.

cycles of their own. They follow the nine- or ten-year cycle of the snowshoe rabbit. As the prey population increases, so does the predator population. As the predators feed on the snowshoe rabbit and reduce its numbers, many of them starve to death because of lack of prey, and so they experience their own population crash.

These population explosions have a serious impact on the food chains. For example, as the number of snowshoe rabbits grows, the amount of plants eaten greatly increases. But there is only so much plant food in one area. Eventually, the rabbits have eaten it all, cutting down the food supply for future generations.

Scientists have discovered another factor that helps to limit runaway animal populations. For instance, the snowshoe rabbit's liver, which normally stores an animal starch called glycogen, does not work properly when the rabbit experiences stress from overcrowding. Glycogen is easily changed to glucose, the sugar that animals use for a source of energy. When snowshoe rabbits are overcrowded, their livers do not store as much glycogen as usual. Instead of running away from predators, the rabbits with damaged livers lack energy. They may lie down and die before the predator has even reached them.

After the population crash, the few survivors find themselves in a world with plenty of room and plenty of food. Soon the predator population is in balance with the prey population, and gradually they build up their numbers again.

chapter four

Food Energy in Pyramids

In the early 1920s, the British ecologist Charles S. Elton spent a summer studying the feeding habits of foxes on an arctic island. He counted all the small animals and birds that were eaten by a fox, and the insects and worms that were eaten by the small animals. He noticed that the total numbers of the different animals formed a pyramid.

Going up the food chain, from the producers to the primary, secondary, and tertiary consumers, the number of organisms decreased. The producers were at the bottom of the pyramid, which consisted of millions of plants. The second level of the pyramid included the primary consumers, which consisted of thousands of insects and worms. The third level of the pyramid included the secondary consumers, which consisted of hundreds of small animals. The fox was at the fourth level, which included the tertiary consumers and had the smallest number of organisms.

Feeding relationships among organisms at different trophic levels can be illustrated in what is known as ecological pyramids. They are also sometimes called Eltonian pyramids, in honor of the importance of Elton's contributions to the science of ecology.

The Pyramid of Numbers

The pyramid-shaped relationship among the number of organisms at each trophic level is known as a pyramid of numbers. This kind of pyramid arrangement worked well for the ecosystem Elton studied, but in some cases, the numbers

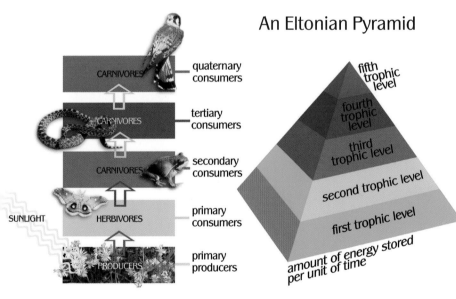

The organisms in a food chain form a pyramid. The bottom level represents the producers, which usually have the largest numbers and total weight. The other levels are primary, secondary, tertiary, and quaternary consumers. The numbers and total weight of these organisms decrease with each step up the pyramid.

The ecosystem in a redwood forest does not follow a neat pyramid, since just a few redwood trees support a large number of insects.

of organisms do not form such a neat pyramid. In a redwood forest, for example, a few trees could provide food for huge numbers of insects, which in turn would support smaller numbers of birds and other carnivores. The upper levels of the pyramid of numbers would thus show the usual shape, but the base—instead of being the largest—would be small. The trophic relationships could be described more accurately by considering the organisms in terms of their weight, rather than of their numbers.

The Pyramid of Biomass

At first, Elton thought that the total weight of the organisms at any one level of the pyramid would be

Food Chains

equal to the weight of those at any other level. A fox, for example, weighs much more than the individual rabbits, mice, and birds that it eats, but it eats so many of them that their total weight is substantial. However, when Elton calculated the weight, or biomass, of all the organisms at each level, he was surprised to find that they were not equal. The biomass also decreased with each step up the trophic levels—so there was also a pyramid of biomass. The fox ate much more than its own weight of rabbits, mice, and birds. They, in turn, consumed more than their own weight in insects, seeds, and other foods; and the insects ate more than their own weight in plant food.

What happens to the biomass that is lost from one level to the next higher one? When a fox eats a rabbit, for instance, it does not eat the rabbit's entire body. It may eat only the meat, leaving the skin and bones. Part of the

The pyramid of biomass shows that when one animal consumes another, such as a fox eating a rabbit, only part of the consumed animal's biomass transfers to the consumer. Part of the rabbit is uneaten by the fox and is left as waste for scavengers.

meat consumed may not be digested and leaves the fox's body as waste products. The wastes and leftovers are then eaten by scavengers. Part of the food eaten goes to build biomass for the growing fox. Another part is used for energy for the animal's activities, such as moving, breathing, digesting, and reproducing. Thus, only a small part of the rabbit's biomass is actually converted to fox biomass.

The Pyramid of Energy

If we think of the organisms at each trophic level in terms of the energy they contain rather than their weight, we find that the energy relationships form a pyramid of energy. This pyramid demonstrates why a large biomass of little animals supports a smaller biomass of big animals.

All living things get energy from food. The energy stored in foods is measured in units called calories. A calorie is the amount of heat needed to raise the temperature of one gram of water by one degree centigrade. (The "calorie" used as a measure of foods' energy content is actually a kilocalorie—1,000 calories.) When a fox eats a rabbit, food energy from the rabbit is transferred and stored in the fox's body. But when the fox uses energy to run, for instance, a lot of the energy is lost as heat.

Since organisms use up energy when they move, reproduce, eliminate wastes, and grow, they cannot pass on all the energy they have eaten in the form of food.

Each level of this woodland energy pyramid represents the amount of energy stored at that level. At the base are the producers where most of the energy from the sun is stored, such as trees and plants. The other levels represent consumers, including (second from bottom) *a caterpillar eating a leaf,* (second from top) *a blue tit bird feeding its offspring,* and (top) *a peregrine falcon eating a bird.* Each level contains less energy than the one below it.

In fact, studies of various ecosystems indicated that in general, only about 10 percent of the energy in any trophic level is transferred to organisms in the next higher trophic level. This is called the "10 percent rule." For example, to gain 1 pound (0.5 kg), a person would have to eat about 10 pounds (4.5 kg) of bass. The bass would need to eat 100 pounds (45 kg) of

Picky Eaters

Most people would be afraid if a great white shark swam past them in the ocean. Studies have shown, however, that the great white shark is actually a picky eater and does not really live up to its man-eating reputation. According to Dr. A. Peter Klimley, a biologist at the University of California Bodega Marine Laboratory, great white sharks prefer to feed on animals such as seals and whales, which contain energy-rich layers of fat. Humans and sea otters are too lean. Fat has more than twice the energy value of muscle. Since great white sharks have very slow digestion, they are less likely to waste their time feeding on anything that does not give them the energy they need in a short amount of time.

minnows. The minnows would need 1,000 pounds (450 kg) of water fleas, and the water fleas would need to feed on 10,000 pounds (4,500 kg) of algae. More recent studies have shown, however, that the 10 percent rule is not always an accurate guide to the transfer of energy in nature. Instead, in real-life food webs, the efficiency of energy transfer may be as low as 0.05 percent or as high as 20 percent.

Only a small amount of energy gets passed on to other trophic levels, so there are usually no more than four or five links in a food chain. At the bottom of the food web are the producers, the largest population group. Next come the primary consumers, which must eat large numbers of producers to get enough energy to function and grow. Going up each level of the pyramid, less and less energy is available. The number of organisms the pyramid can support is smaller. This explains why there are typically more prey than predators in a community. Thus, the pyramid of numbers, the pyramid of biomass, and the pyramid of energy all describe relationships among organisms in a single ecosystem.

chapter five

How Nature Recycles

What materials does your community recycle?

Newspapers, glass bottles, aluminum cans, and

plastics? We tend to think of recycling programs as

something developed rather recently, when people

became aware of the problems our "throwaway

society" was creating for the environment.

Actually, though, recycling has always been a part of our world. Some of the air molecules you breathe may have passed through the lungs of Caesar or Shakespeare or some other famous person of the past. Some of the calcium in your bones may once have been part of a dinosaur's skeleton or the shell of some ancient sea creature.

All living things need certain chemical elements, or essential nutrients, to grow and maintain themselves properly. These nutrients can be found in the soil, the water, or the atmosphere. Energy from the sun flows through ecosystems on Earth, passes from one trophic level to the next, and disappears in the environment in the process. But Earth does not receive a continuous supply of chemical elements from anywhere. They cannot be produced or used up but are passed around from the environment to living

A forklift moves bails of plastic bottles at the San Francisco Recycling Center. Since most bottled water is consumed away from home where recycling isn't an option, an estimated 40 million bottles a day go into the trash.

organisms and back again. The same essential nutrients must be used over and over. This kind of nutrient recycling, which usually involves both living things and Earth, is known as a biogeochemical cycle, from bio, meaning "living" and geo, meaning "earth."

All nutrients in an ecosystem must go through biogeochemical cycles. These cycles and the food chains are linked in many complex ways. For instance, plants take carbon dioxide from the air and water and minerals from the soil, and using energy from the sun, they make food through photo–synthesis. The animals that feed on the plants use some of the nutrients for growth, daily activities, and reproduction.

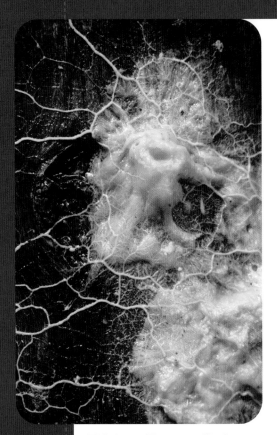

The plant materials that cannot be used by the animals are eliminated as waste products, the elements of which are returned to the environment by decomposers. Animals that eat other animals in turn use some of the nutrients for their own growth, daily activities, and reproduction. When the plants and animals die, decomposers break down the organic material and return the nutrients to the soil and air. Thus, most of the food produced by plants is eventually broken down into carbon dioxide, water, and

This log will eventually decay and return to the soil, thanks to decomposers such as the slime mold covering it.

minerals and returned to the ecosystem for reuse by other living things.

The Water Cycle

Probably the most familiar and visible biogeochemical cycle is the water cycle. Water evaporates from the surface of rivers, streams, lakes, and oceans. When

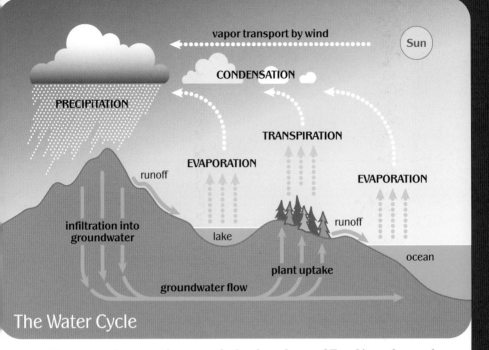

The Water Cycle

vapor transport by wind

Sun

CONDENSATION

PRECIPITATION

TRANSPIRATION

EVAPORATION

runoff

EVAPORATION

infiltration into groundwater

lake

runoff

ocean

plant uptake

groundwater flow

Nature recycles water between the lands and seas of Earth's surface and the water vapor in the atmosphere. Evaporation and precipitation are important parts of the cycle. Plants and animals also play a major role.

weather conditions are right, the water vapor in clouds can condense into liquid water, which falls to the surface as rain. Some of the rainwater then falls on land areas and drains off into streams, rivers, and eventually into the ocean.

Some of the rain is absorbed by the soil and drawn up through the roots of plants. Water pressure in the stems and leaves helps to keep plants sturdy—it is the only "skeleton" that some plants have. But plants continually lose water through tiny openings in their leaves, so they need a new supply. (If you forget to water a houseplant in a pot, it soon droops and wilts.)

Animals (including humans) are another important part of nature's water cycle. They drink water and also take in moisture in juicy fruits and leaves of plants. Your own body is really about two-thirds water. Animals lose some of their body water when they get rid of their body wastes, and there is water vapor in the breath they exhale. When an animal dies, the rest of its body water is returned to the cycle.

The Nitrogen Cycle

Nature also recycles important chemical elements. Nitrogen, for example, is a gas that makes up 78 percent of Earth's atmosphere. Most plants and animals cannot use pure nitrogen gas, yet it is a part of many important body chemicals. A key link in the nitrogen cycle is played by specialized bacteria that live in the soil or in plant roots. These nitrogen fixers change nitrogen gas into chemical forms that plants can use. The plants further change these simple nitrogen compounds into proteins and other complex substances. Animals get the nitrogen compounds they need by eating plants or other animals.

When animals and plants die, decay bacteria break down the complex nitrogen compounds in their bodies into simpler substances, such

Did You Know?

The air over 1 acre (0.4 hectare) of land contains about 35,000 tons (32,000 metric tons) of nitrogen.

as water and the strong-smelling gas ammonia. Other bacteria carry the process further to produce nitrogen gas. This is the reverse of the nitrogen-fixing chemical reactions, and it completes the cycle, returning nitrogen to the atmosphere.

The natural nitrogen cycle is perfectly balanced. The nitrogen removed from the soil by plants and animals is completely replaced by the nitrogen-fixing bacteria and the decay processes.

Animals, plants, and bacteria all contribute to nature's recycling of nitrogen. Nitrogen gas in the atmosphere is converted to forms that living things can use. It is then returned to the atmosphere when wastes and dead matter decompose.

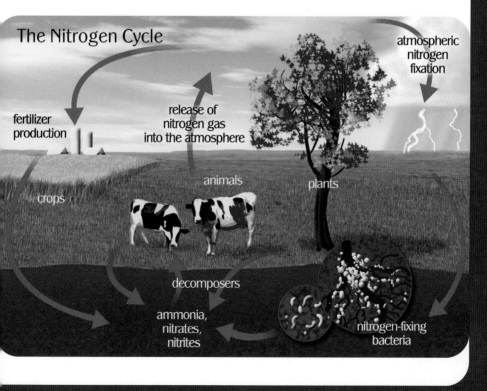

The Nitrogen Cycle

atmospheric nitrogen fixation

fertilizer production

release of nitrogen gas into the atmosphere

animals

plants

crops

decomposers

ammonia, nitrates, nitrites

nitrogen-fixing bacteria

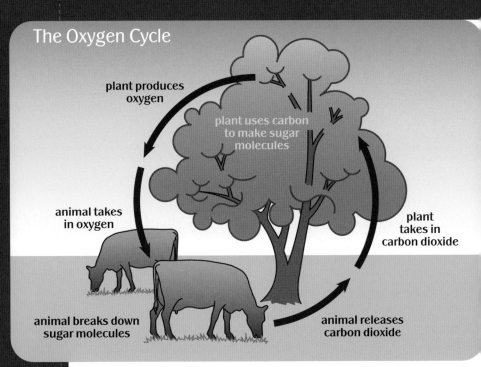

The Oxygen Cycle

plant produces oxygen

plant uses carbon to make sugar molecules

animal takes in oxygen

plant takes in carbon dioxide

animal breaks down sugar molecules

animal releases carbon dioxide

Both animals and plants need to take in oxygen, but the amount of this gas in the atmosphere stays the same because of nature's recycling processes. Photosynthesis replaces the oxygen that living things use up.

The Oxygen Cycle

Living animals and plants play key roles in the recycling of another important element, oxygen. Although this gas makes up close to 21 percent of Earth's atmosphere, scientists believe that there was practically none of it in the air when our planet was first formed. At that time, billions of years ago, Earth's oxygen was mainly bound up in chemical compounds, in the water of the oceans, and in rocks and minerals. For the first living things, oxygen was a deadly poison. But gradually creatures appeared that could make oxygen less poisonous or even use it to generate energy.

Eventually there were plants that not only used oxygen but also produced it. During photosynthesis, as plants use sunlight energy to combine carbon dioxide and water into food materials, oxygen gas is released as a by-product. All the oxygen in Earth's atmosphere was formed by plants and photosynthesizing microorganisms. The microscopic algae that float on the ocean's surface in our present-day world, as well as trees, grasses, and other land plants, help to supply oxygen to the atmosphere.

Animals cannot produce oxygen, but they are heavy consumers of this important gas. They use it in respiration, a process somewhat like a fire burning, in which complex chemicals are combined with oxygen to release energy. Land animals obtain the oxygen they need by breathing air. Water dwellers use the oxygen dissolved in the water. Plants "breathe" too, but the amount of oxygen their respiration uses up is generally far smaller than the amount they produce in photosynthesis. So in the natural oxygen cycle, plants add oxygen to the atmosphere, while animals use it up.

The Carbon Cycle

The carbon cycle is interlocked with the oxygen cycle. The connecting link between these two cycles is carbon dioxide, which is formed when the carbon compounds combine with oxygen—either in a burning fire or in respiration. Proteins, sugars, fats, and many other complex substances that are found in the bodies of plants and animals all contain carbon. This

Fossil fuels, such as coal, contain carbon. Coal is the largest single source of fuel for the generation of electricity world-wide. The carbon cycle plays a vital role for all living things.

element is also a major part of the fossil fuels: coal, oil, and gas, which were formed from the remains of ancient plant and animal life.

There is not much carbon dioxide in Earth's atmosphere, compared to the amounts of nitrogen and oxygen—only 0.035 percent. But this gas is very

Food Chains

important for living things. It is the main raw material of photosynthesis. Thus, it is the ultimate source of all food for our planet's creatures.

Carbon dioxide from the atmosphere may be carried down into streams and rivers by the rain, or it may dissolve directly into the surface waters of lakes and oceans. (Earth's oceans contain sixty times as much carbon dioxide as there is in the atmosphere.) The tiny plants that float on the ocean surface in huge numbers use some of the dissolved carbon

Burning of fuels and the respiration of animals and plants send carbon dioxide into the atmosphere. Plants and algae capture this carbon dioxide and use it to build food materials, which may be eaten by animals. Scientists believe that Earth's carbon cycle is no longer perfectly balanced.

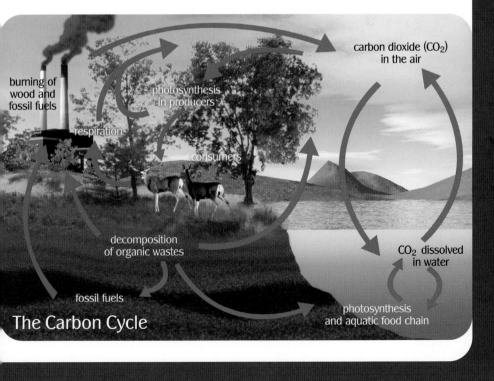

carbon dioxide (CO_2) in the air

burning of wood and fossil fuels

photosynthesis in producers

respiration

consumers

decomposition of organic wastes

CO_2 dissolved in water

fossil fuels

photosynthesis and aquatic food chain

The Carbon Cycle

dioxide in photosynthesis and play a major role in producing oxygen gas. But some of these microscopic creatures use carbon dioxide in forming hard protective shells around their delicate bodies. When they die, they sink to the bottom, taking some of the carbon out of circulation.

Animals and plants that build carbon into their body chemicals also take this element out of circulation—at least temporarily. But when they die and their bodies are broken down, the carbon they contained is recycled. Carbon compounds in rocks may also be returned to circulation when they are dissolved out by rainwater or vaporized by erupting volcanoes.

The Phosphorus Cycle

Many mineral elements from the soil are important for living organisms. They are taken in by plants and pass up the food chains to animals. One of the most important of these minerals is the chemical element phosphorus. This element is a key part of DNA and RNA, the chemicals of heredity. Phosphorus is also part of a compound called ATP (adenosine triphosphate). Living things use ATP to store the energy they need to keep handy for the work that goes on constantly inside their cells.

Phosphorus is found in rocks in compounds called phosphates, in which it is linked with oxygen. Rain that soaks into the soil dissolves out some of the phosphates from the bits of rock. Plant roots take in

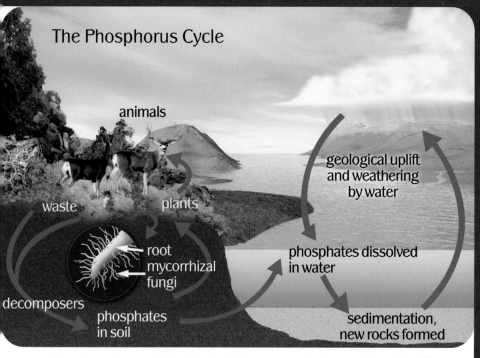

The Phosphorus Cycle

animals

plants

waste

decomposers

root
mycorrhizal
fungi

phosphates
in soil

geological uplift
and weathering
by water

phosphates dissolved
in water

sedimentation,
new rocks formed

Phosphorus from rocks is dissolved by water and taken up from the soil by plants. It is passed on to animals that eat the plants, then returned to the soil by decomposers. Phosphorus is one of many important chemicals in living things.

dissolved phosphates together with the water they absorb. The plants build phosphorus into their chemicals. It then is passed on to the animals that eat the plants. Decomposers working on the body wastes of living organisms and the bodies of dead ones return phosphorus to the soil.

Phosphorus recycling does not work perfectly, however. Some of the phosphates returned to the soil are carried by rainwater into streams and rivers and eventually washed away to sea. There they form hard rocky deposits on the ocean bottom. Sewage-disposal systems built by humans carry phosphorus-rich wastes directly into Earth's water

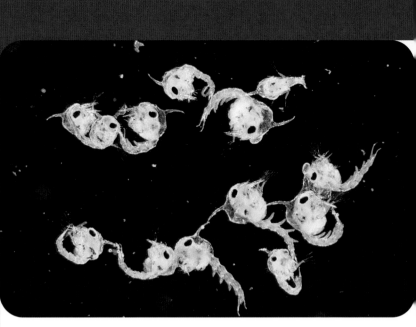

Tiny animal plankton like these found in the ocean play an important role in the phosphorus cycle.

systems. Not only body wastes but also detergents used to wash clothes and dishes contain phosphorus. About 3.5 million tons (3.2 million metric tons) of phosphorus are carried away by the rivers each year. Not all of this is lost, though. Some of the phosphorus that washes into the ocean is taken up by phytoplankton, the tiny single-celled plant-like organisms that live in the surface waters. It then passes up the ocean food chains as the phytoplankton are eaten by tiny animals, which are prey for larger sea dwellers. Some of the phosphorus is returned to the land in the bodies of fish caught for food and in small amounts in bird droppings, or guano.

Various other minerals are also needed by living organisms. In some cases, the amounts needed are so small they can barely be measured, yet they are essential for health and life. The food chains help to distribute them among Earth's creatures and eventually return them to the environment. All the biogeochemical cycles are connected to one another and are vital to all living things on Earth. The constant recycling of nutrients makes it possible for ecosystems to exist over extremely long periods of time.

chapter six

What happens when a toxic substance or a foreign species invades an ecosystem? Just one tiny change in an environment can result in a series of chain reactions, in which the food chains play a major role.

Take the case of DDT, for example. This pesticide was considered a miracle when it was introduced in the 1940s. In less developed countries, especially in the tropics, it saved the lives of millions of people by killing the mosquitoes that spread malaria. Larger crop production resulted from DDT's destruction of insect pests. The increased food supply saved even more people from starvation. DDT was so powerful and long lasting that only one application was needed. People were not yet aware of the damaging effects this "amazing" pesticide was going to have on the complex web of life.

In the mid 1950s, the World Health Organization sprayed DDT on the island of Borneo to eliminate malaria. Soon side effects of DDT started to appear. DDT killed not only the mosquitoes but also other insects, such as flies and cockroaches, that lived in the people's houses. Caterpillars that fed on the thatched roofs of woven leaves and straw were unaffected by the pesticide. The wasps that normally preyed on the caterpillars

Crops were regularly dusted with DDT before its danger was known. DDT contamination affected many food chains.

were killed, however. When the wasps were no longer present, the caterpillar population soon rose out of control and caused the roofs to collapse.

Gecko lizards also lived in the houses and ate the dead bodies of the flies and cockroaches. Since DDT cannot be broken down and tends to accumulate in the fatty tissues of organisms, geckos died from the poison concentrated in the insect bodies. Village cats fed on the gecko lizards and also died from DDT poisoning. Once the cats were eliminated, the rat population overran the island. Fleas that lived on the rats were carriers of a disease called sylvatic plague, which could be transmitted to humans. New cats were then flown to different parts of the island to reduce the rat population and help bring things back to normal.

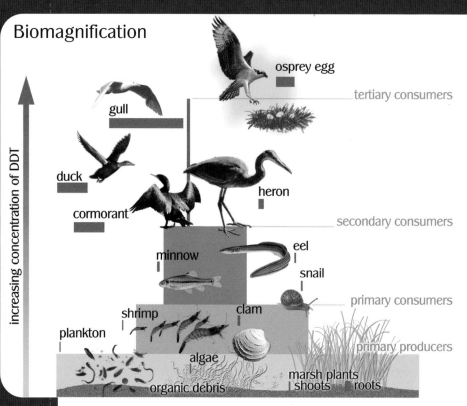

Biomagnification

increasing concentration of DDT

tertiary consumers

osprey egg

gull

duck

cormorant

heron

secondary consumers

minnow

eel

snail

primary consumers

shrimp

clam

plankton

primary producers

algae

marsh plants
shoots   roots

organic debris

This marshland food web shows how chemicals can get more and more concentrated at each step up the food chains. DDT sprayed on crops is washed by rain into streams that empty into the nearby marsh and bay. Bottom-living animals and plants pick it up and then are eaten by fish and other water animals. Birds that feed on the fish have the highest DDT levels in their bodies.

Ecologists often use ecological pyramids to illustrate how toxic chemicals in the environment can gradually accumulate in the bodies of the organisms in an ecosystem. This effect, known as bioconcentration, explains how a toxic chemical may build to a level high enough to kill the organism. Bio-concentration may also lead to biological magnification, the increasing concentration of a toxin as it moves up the trophic levels of a food chain.

For instance, when DDT was widely used, runoff from fields contaminated streams, rivers, and oceans with DDT. The algae growing in these waters absorbed the DDT. When tiny aquatic animals ate the algae, the DDT was passed along the food chain. Larger fish ate these poisoned smaller fish, and DDT accumulated in their bodies.

At each higher trophic level, the concentration of DDT increased. When a large fish ate many small fish contaminated with DDT, a huge dose of DDT accumulated in the large fish's body because of the number of poisoned fish it had eaten.

DDT weakened the shell of this peregrine falcon egg on the right, versus the normal egg on the left.

When birds ate the larger fish, the DDT was concentrated further. It did not kill the birds directly, but it reduced the amount of calcium in the shells of eggs the female birds laid. The eggshells were so weak that they broke when the parent birds sat on them.

A number of bird species, including peregrine falcons, ospreys, brown pelicans, American eagles, and the California condor, lost whole generations of chicks and were in danger of becoming extinct. DDT is so persistent in the environment that long after it was banned in the United States in 1972, birds continued to lay contaminated eggs.

Hormone Pollutants

In the early 1990s, British biologists noticed something strange about the fish they had taken out of the sewage-filled River Lee near London—the reproductive organs of the males, the testes, were covered with eggs. But eggs are normally produced by females in their reproductive organs, the ovaries. Scientists believed that something in the water was acting as a sex hormone and was interfering with reproductive development. Two studies on this phenomenon were conducted. A study sponsored by the U.S. Geological Survey showed that fish living in streams in the United States also appear to have unusual levels of sex hormones. In another survey, British researchers suggested that it was not industrial chemicals that disrupted the fishes' reproductive development. Natural hormones, estrogens, in women's urine may be responsible. In addition, both studies seemed to show that the fish found in polluted waters were more likely to have abnormal levels of hormones than those found in cleaner waters.

In a more intensive study at sewage-contaminated waters of Lake Mead near Las Vegas, Nevada, the researchers also found that the male fish had unusually high levels of vitellogenin. This protein is involved in egg-laying that normally occurs only in females. In another study, sponsored by the U.K. Environmental Agency, British researchers collected sewage from three treatment plants and managed to isolate the compounds that were likely to act like estrogens in the fish. The researchers discovered that these compounds were not industrial chemicals. They were three hormones found in women—17b-estradiol, estrone, and ethynyl estradiol. This last one, which was found in small amounts, is a strong synthetic hormone in birth control pills.

These concentrations of hormone pollutants increase as they move up the food chain. The Florida panther, for instance, consumes a strong dose of the hormone pollutants when it feeds on raccoons that eat contaminated fish. Some scientists believe that this contamination has been responsible for various reproductive problems in Florida panthers. Other species, such as alligators, have also experienced the effects of hormone pollutants. In 1980 there was an accidental spill of dicofol, a pesticide, in Lake Apopka in Florida—the home of many alligators. Scientists believe that this hormonelike pollutant damages the reproductive systems of alligators. As a result, there has been a 90 percent reduction in the number of young alligators in the lake.

Hormone pollutants, which can affect reproductive systems, have reduced the number of young alligators in Florida's Lake Apopka.

Animal Invaders

People are becoming more and more aware of the dangerous effects that pesticides and other pollutants have on wildlife and humans. Desperately wanting to find a safe way to eliminate pests without harming other living things, biologists have tried to take a more natural route—fighting nature with nature. Scientists call this biological pest control. Instead of using chemicals, they bring in foreign species that prey on certain pests and let nature take its course.

For instance, an Australian tree called the melaleuca was introduced into the United States in the late 1800s. In Florida it was used to help dry out the ground around the Everglades. It was too successful, though. It has been spreading through the forests at a rate of 35 to 50 acres (14 to 20 hectares) a day. The melaleuca has become an environmental hazard, forcing out the

The melaleuca, an Australian tree, has displaced many native plants in the Florida Everglades.

native plants and causing problems for electrical equipment and power lines. In May 1997, the U.S. Department of Agriculture released snout beetles imported from Australia into the Florida Everglades to control the melaleuca's growth. The snout beetle eats only the melaleuca and prefers the tree's new leaves and flower buds. Scientists hope this will keep the melaleuca from spreading.

Unexpected Poisons

In the 1930s, midwesterners were alarmed when their valued lake trout began disappearing from the Great Lakes. It was believed that the sea lamprey, which looks like an eel and preys on lake trout, was responsible for the decline of the fish population. Biologists then released chemicals that would reduce the lamprey population and were thought to be harmless to the rest of the marine life. Studies have shown, however, that the lake trout may have been poisoned. Scientists noticed that the lake trout's dramatic decline started about the same time that large amounts of dioxins, polychlorinated biphenyls (PCBs), and other chemicals were poured into the lake.

Similar biological control efforts have been successful, but there have also been some disasters. For example, in the 1930s, the poisonous cane toad was brought into Australia to get rid of a beetle that was destroying sugarcane crops. However, the beetles fly only at night, and the toads, which are active during the day, were unable to eat them. The toads started to invade the land, and 102 toads became a trillion.

In 1992 scientists had evidence suggesting that lake trout embryos exposed to dioxins could develop a deadly disease called blue sac syndrome and that future generations would not survive. Restocking dioxin-free lake trout in the Great Lakes has produced some improvement in the population. But laboratory tests indicate that less-than-lethal amounts of dioxin-like pollutants may still cause harm to the fish. In 1995 the EPA established limits on discharges of about forty toxic chemicals, including DDT and PCBs, into the Great Lakes.

Lake trout are very important in the food web. They are one of the top predators in the Great Lakes and keep the numbers of smaller fish under control. As the lake trout disappeared, other fish have overrun the waters and have begun a chain reaction among other species in the aquatic ecosystem.

Bringing a strange species into a new habitat is always a risk. It seems that no matter how familiar scientists become with an ecosystem, it is hard to predict what will happen when a foreign species is released into it.

In biological pest control, scientists can control what species are introduced into a habitat, but they cannot control the effects. Sometimes, however, animals invade habitats on their own—and the effects on the environment can be disastrous.

Scientists think that many animals invade new ecosystems by stowing away in a ship's ballast water.

The European green crab made its way from the shores of the East Coast to the West Coast. It is threatening the food chains in the waters from San Francisco to the Pacific Northwest.

Ballast water is used to stabilize cargo ships. When the water is pumped into a ship, it carries many different organisms. The organisms are then released into new surroundings when the ship docks and dumps the ballast water.

When an animal or plant invades new territories, it can cause serious problems for the environment and the species living in it. Consider the European green crab. It has lived in the waters off the eastern shores of North America for about 180 years. By the late 1980s, the crab had made its way to the West Coast, where it was found in the San Francisco Bay. It is probable that the crab came to San Francisco in ballast waters or in bait shipments. The green crab has an insatiable appetite and feeds on oysters, clams, and other crab species. It is not only threatening the commercial shellfisheries in the Pacific Northwest. But it may have disastrous effects on the food chain as well. Scientists are concerned that birds may have to compete with the green crabs for food and that this may result in a decline in the bird population.

chapter seven

Humans and Food Chains

During the 1950s and 1960s, aboveground nuclear-

weapons testing took place at the Nevada Test Site,

north of Las Vegas. The test explosions released

many radioactive substances into the environment,

including dangerous isotopes of strontium, cesium,

and iodine. Cows that ate grass or drank water on

which these radioisotopes fell secreted some of the

radioactive materials in their milk.

Researchers at the National Cancer Institute
believe that people who lived in the area during
that time may have been exposed to radioactive
iodine when they drank contaminated milk. The
amount of iodine exposure during the test period
was about two rads (a unit of radiation). This is five
times the amount of radiation a woman gets from a
modern mammogram.

Some researchers think that between ten
thousand and seventy-five thousand children who
were exposed to the radioactive iodine fallout may
develop thyroid cancer sometime during their lives.
Others feel that since thyroid tumors associated with

radiation overdose usually show up within about twenty-five years, cancers caused by the Nevada tests probably would have appeared by now.

Whenever foreign chemicals or poisons enter the environment, they eventually make their way up the food chains and may affect people's lives. Humans are especially vulnerable because we are the top of the food chains, and toxic pollutants usually become more con-centrated as they pass up the trophic levels.

Aboveground testing of nuclear weaponry in the United States (above) *started in the 1940s and was common into the 1960s.*

Pollutants in the Food Chain

Pollution in the environment is an ongoing problem. Health scientists are especially concerned these days about people who eat contaminated fish. Research has shown that the PCBs and other hormone pollutants that are found in many Great Lakes fish have damaged the development of infants and children whose mothers ate these fish. Women who eat contaminated fish may pass the pollutants on to their children before birth and through breastfeeding. Studies have shown that there may be a link between high doses of PCBs in a woman's breast milk and behavioral problems in her newborn.

At Wayne State University in Detroit, Michigan, Sandra and Joseph Jacobson found that pregnant women who ate large amounts of Lake Michigan fish gave birth to babies with lower weight and smaller head circumference than the babies of women who did not eat fish. Also, the babies whose mothers had

Beware of Raw Shellfish

Mollusks, which include shellfish like oysters, clams, and mussels, may be a delicacy for some people. But they may also make people sick if they are eaten raw. Since mollusks cannot move, they eat by filtering water through their bodies, removing nutrients in the process. Unfortunately, they can also take in and store harmful bacteria and viruses that can cause a variety of illnesses. These come from human sewage that contaminates the waters where the mollusks live. When people eat contaminated shellfish raw, they also consume the viruses and bacteria.

the highest levels of PCBs in their blood later scored the lowest on intelligence testing, which included verbal and memory tests. In addition, recent studies at the State University of New York at Oswego found that the newborns of mothers who had eaten Lake Ontario fish had more abnormal reflexes and took longer to calm down after being startled.

Other studies also may suggest an influence of hormonelike pollutants on humans. A 1996 analysis of sperm-count studies in twenty countries seemed to indicate that men are becoming less fertile. This could be the result of an accumulation of pollutants, with effects similar to those of female hormones, taken in through the food chain. However, sperm counts did not decline everywhere. Regional differences in pollution or other factors might be responsible for these findings.

It is not clear if these hormonelike pollutants are a problem for society as a whole or are just isolated cases. More research is needed, but some international organizations agree that there is a problem and that exposure to pollutants should be limited. In 2001 members of the United Nations Economic Commission for Europe (including the United States and Canada) signed an agreement that would eliminate the use of twelve persistent organic pollutants (POPs). POPs are chemicals that remain in the environment for a long time. They can be found throughout the world and build up in the bodies of living organisms. Sometimes called the "dirty dozen," some of the POPs targeted by the agreement include insecticides, such as DDT and chlordane; PCBs; and certain chemical by-products, such as dioxins and furans.

Maintaining a Balance

For millions of years, nature has somehow maintained a balance among all living things. Predator and prey relationships in the wild usually keep animal populations in check. But the human population continues to grow, and so does the amount of food people consume. Many scientists believe that humans are eating more than they need and that there may not be enough food for everyone. They predict that as the number of people on Earth continues to increase, eventually even people in the wealthy nations will not be able to afford to eat much meat. We may all have to feed lower on the food chains,

Health experts say a diet with more plant foods, such as fruits and vegetables, and less fat is healthier for humans.

depending more on grains, vegetables, and fruits for our food energy.

Such a change in diet may not be a bad thing. For years, health experts have been saying we should eat more plant foods and less fat, especially the saturated fat that is found in meat. For many Americans, this would be a dramatic and difficult change

Did You Know?

The average American adult eats more than half a ton (0.5 metric ton) of food each year—and an estimated 20 to 25 percent of Americans weigh at least 20 percent more than is healthy.

in eating habits. But for some people, a diet without meat is already a way of life. These people are called vegetarians.

There are several different kinds of vegetarians. Semi-vegetarians eat dairy foods, eggs, chicken, and fish, but no other animal flesh. Pesco-vegetarians eat dairy foods, eggs, and fish, but no other animal flesh. There are also lacto-ovo-vegetarians, who eat dairy foods and eggs but no other animal flesh. Lacto-vegetarians eat dairy products but no eggs. Ovo-vegetarians eat eggs but no dairy foods or animal flesh. Finally, vegans do not eat any animal foods of any kind. In some parts of the world, vegetarian diets are a cultural tradition—or a necessity if little meat (or money to buy it) is available. A number of people in wealthier nations choose vegetarianism for ethical reasons, because they do not want to be responsible for the killing of animals.

Some health experts believe that vegetarians may be healthier than people who eat animal products. Studies strongly suggest that vegetarians have a lower risk of obesity, hypertension, and heart disease. Some studies indicate that vegetarians may also have a lower risk of colon cancer.

Many vegetarians think they are doing their body good by eliminating fatty meats from their diet and eating only plant foods. A vegetarian diet may not completely fulfill a person's nutritional needs, however. Vegans, the strictest vegetarians, run the greatest risk of nutritional deficiencies. People who eat only plant foods must eat larger amounts of food to get the same amount of energy as a person who eats animal foods. Remember that the energy yield decreases by about 90 percent with each level in the food chain. Moreover, humans use plant foods much less efficiently than do natural herbivores. Our bodies cannot get nourishment from the cellulose found in plants the way animals such as cows can. A cow's stomach contains helpful bacteria that break down the cellulose in the grass that the cow eats. That is why a cow can get more nutritional value from plants than we can. Since humans cannot digest cellulose, plant fibers just pass out with our body wastes, without providing any food energy.

It is hard for vegetarians to get enough of certain vitamins that are plentiful in animal foods but not in plants. Vegetarians may also not get enough protein. Food proteins are digested into smaller molecules called amino acids. The acids are then used as building blocks to make the thousands of proteins we need for growth, repair, and the many activities of our

Take a Bite

Most humans are omnivores. We eat both animal and plant foods. In fact, our long-ago ancestors adapted to an omnivorous diet; our teeth are evidence of this. We can eat a wider variety of foods than most other animals because we have four different kinds of teeth. The sharp, chisel-shaped incisors in the front act like knives to slice and bite off chunks of food. They work like the incisors that herbivores use to clip off grass or other plant leaves. Next to the incisors are the canines. Like the slashing fangs of carnivores, our pointed canines are used to tear food into bits. Next come the premolars, double-pointed teeth that work like the blades of scissors to cut food. They also help the molars, broad teeth with raised bumps and ridges, to crush and grind food into a smooth pulp, the way the premolars and molars of herbivores grind up grains and plant fibers.

individual cells. Our bodies can make some amino acids from sugars and other nutrients. But there are others that we need for building proteins but cannot make on our own. We have to get these essential amino acids from foods.

Most animal foods, such as meat, poultry, fish, eggs, cheese, and milk, contain all the essential amino acids. The food proteins from these animal sources are called complete proteins. A few kinds of plant proteins are complete too.

Soybean products such as tofu have proteins that are very much like animal proteins and contain all the essential amino acids.

Most plant proteins, however, are not complete. They contain only small amounts of one or more essential amino acids. The proteins in foods such as legumes (beans and peas), nuts, seeds, grains, and vegetables are all incomplete proteins. Just one of these foods cannot supply all our protein needs by itself, but certain combinations of plant foods—such as rice and beans—can together supply all the essential amino acids. To eat a healthy, balanced diet,

For a healthy diet, vegetarians eat a variety of fruits and vegetables. They also eat rice and beans, which combine to supply necessary protein.

Food Chains

vegetarians must be especially careful to eat a variety of foods. The more varied the diet, nutrition experts advise, the better the chances of getting all the nutrients we need.

As for everybody else—moderation is the key. Meat in the diet can be healthy and nutritious, but overconsumption can cause problems.

Learning for the Future

We have seen how pollution can have serious effects on the food chain. Ecologists are trying to think of ways to eliminate pollutants in the ecosystem. In November 1996, ecologist George Chan began a very interesting experiment on the largest island of Fiji, in the South Pacific. Chan is a strong supporter of integrated farming. This method uses the waste products of one agricultural industry as fertilizer or fuel for another, which in turn adds little or no pollution to the environment. He worked with the help of students from the Montfort Boys' Town, a boys' school on the island.

Fiji has an established fish-farming industry. But fishing is in jeopardy because of brewery waste dumping—more than 14 million cubic feet (400,000 cubic meters) each year. The brewery waste has covered some of the coral reefs and destroyed much of the local sea life. Moreover, many Fiji residents eat fish contaminated by the harmful waste. To combat this problem, Chan used the waste as fertilizer for mushrooms. As the mushrooms grew, they produced a residue. Normally, this residue would have been dumped on fields. There it fertilizes crops but also causes an overflow of muck. At Montfort, however, the residue was used as food

Fish farming and other controlled environments for raising food may be one way to eliminate pollutants from the ecosystem. This fish farm is in Spain.

for chickens, pigs, and other animals. Since it is both nutritious and safe, it made an excellent slop, or feed.

Animal wastes were then put into a contraption called the decomposer, where the chemicals in the wastes separated. During this process, methane gas was released and collected in a compartment at the top of the device. The solid or liquid wastes settled to the bottom. Usually, the methane would have been released into the atmosphere and lost. But in the Fiji project, it was bottled and used to operate a gas generator to power the lights of the school, or it was sold.

Food Chains

Meanwhile, the solid matter left in the decomposer went through a process that got rid of some of its bacteria at each stage. This eliminated some of its potential to cause illnesses. The decontaminated manure was then converted into nutrients such as nitrogen, phosphorus, and potash. These nutrients are normally used as fertilizer for farming. It was then put into several cleansing ponds, where bacteria, plankton, and other micro-scavengers ate all the unwanted, leftover parts of the original animal wastes. In the final stage, this matter became food for the farmed fish.

The nutrients in the fish pond water were used for growing flowers, strawberries, and vegetables floating on top of the pond, reducing the amount of muck left for disposal. The

The coral reefs near Fiji are healthier because of the effects of George Chan's integrated farming project.

produce was harvested for public consumption, leaving little or no waste at the farm. Chan's integrated farming was very productive for the Montfort Boys' Town. It required less money than traditional farming and brought income to the poor town. Meanwhile, the project helped to clean up the coral reefs.

There is much that the world at large can learn from this small experiment in applied ecology. A thorough, in-depth study of the complex ways our planet's living organisms are linked in food chains and webs can provide insights into how humans can live in harmony with our world, providing for our own needs while preserving resources for future generations.

Glossary

alkaloids: poisonous chemicals made by some plants, ants, and other organisms

amino acids: the chemical building blocks of proteins

ATP: adenosine triphosphate—a chemical compound used by living organisms for the temporary storage of energy

autotrophs: producers; the basis of all food chains, which produce food by photosynthesis or chemosynthesis

batrachotoxin: a deadly poison made by the poison dart frogs of Colombia

bioconcentration: the accumulation of high concentrations of poisons or other chemicals from foods in the bodies of animals that eat them

biodiversity: the variety of species at each trophic level in an ecosystem

biogeochemical cycle: recycling of nutrients between living organisms and Earth's physical environment

biological community: the organisms that live together in the same area

biological magnification: an increase in the concentration of a poison at successively higher trophic levels of a food chain

biological pest control: the use of a pest organism's natural enemies (such as predators or parasites) to control its population

biomass: the total weight of the organisms in a particular area

calorie: the amount of heat needed to raise the temperature of 0.04 ounce (1 gram) of water 1°C

carnivores: animals that eat other animals

cellulose: a fibrous substance in plant cells that humans cannot digest

chemosynthesis: food production by living organisms using energy stored in chemical compounds

chlorophyll: a green pigment in plants and certain bacteria that absorbs sunlight energy

consumers: organisms that eat other organisms in the community

decomposers: organisms that break down wastes and dead matter, returning their components to the environment

dioxins: chlorine-containing hydrocarbons that are toxic by-products of the manufacture of pesticides and are common pollutants in lakes and other waters

ecological pyramids: pyramid-shaped diagrams showing the relative numbers, biomass (weight), or energy content of organisms at different trophic levels in an ecosystem; also called Eltonian pyramids

ecology: the science dealing with the interdependent relationships among organisms and their habitat

ecosystem: a biological community in which organisms live and interact with one another and their environment

essential amino acids: the amino acids that humans cannot produce and must obtain from food

estrogens: hormones found in women and in synthetic birth control pills that may disrupt fishes' reproductive development

food chain: a sequence of organisms, each of which is eaten by the next member in the chain

food web: the interconnected food chains in an ecosystem

herbivores: animals that eat mainly plants

heterotrophs: organisms that cannot make their own food and feed on other organisms or their products. They include consumers and decomposers.

integrated farming: a method using the waste products of one agricultural industry as fertilizer or fuel for another, resulting in minimal pollution of the environment

keystone species: a species essential for the survival of a particular biological community

lacto-ovo-vegetarian: related to a diet including dairy foods and eggs but no other animal flesh

niche: the specific role of an organism in a community, its place in the ecosystem or way of living

nitrogen fixers: bacteria that convert nitrogen gas from the atmosphere to nitrogen compounds that can be used by plants

omnivores: animals that eat both plants and animals

ovo-vegetarian: related to a diet including eggs but no dairy foods or animal flesh

pesco-vegetarian: related to a diet including dairy foods, eggs, and fish, but no other animal flesh

pesticide: poisonous chemical used to kill or control insects or other pest organisms

photosynthesis: a process in which living organisms use sunlight energy to make carbohydrates from carbon dioxide and water, producing oxygen as a by-product

phytoplankton: single-celled plantlike organisms that live in the surface waters of the oceans

polychlorinated biphenyls (PCBs): toxic industrial by-products that are common water pollutants

predators: animals that hunt and kill other animals for food. They are secondary, or higher-level, consumers.

prey: animals that are killed by other animals for food. They include primary consumers and some secondary consumers.

primary consumer: an organism that feeds on a primary producer; also called a first-level consumer, usually a herbivore

primary producer: the first link in a food chain, which directly or indirectly provides food for the whole chain

producers: organisms that make their own food and provide food for other organisms in the ecosystem

pyramid of biomass: pyramid-shaped diagram showing the relative biomass (weight) of organisms at different trophic levels in an ecosystem

pyramid of energy: pyramid-shaped diagram showing the relative energy content of organisms at different trophic levels in an ecosystem

pyramid of numbers: pyramid-shaped diagram showing the relative numbers of organisms at different levels in an ecosystem

quaternary consumer: an organism that feeds on a tertiary consumer; also called a fourth-level consumer

rad: a unit of radiation, calculated according to the amount of energy absorbed by living tissue

respiration: a process in living cells in which carbohydrates and other organic carbon compounds react with oxygen, releasing energy and producing carbon dioxide as a waste product

scavengers: animals that feed on dead animals or wastes of other organisms

secondary consumer: organism that feeds on a primary consumer; also called a second-level consumer; usually a carnivore or an omnivore

semi-vegetarian: related to a diet including dairy foods, eggs, chicken, and fish, but no other animal flesh

tertiary consumer: an organism that feeds on a secondary consumer; also called a third-level consumer

trophic levels: feeding level; the position of a link in a food chain relative to the other links

umbrella species: a species whose preservation will also protect the other members of its biological community

vegan: related to a diet consisting only of plant foods, with no animal foods of any kind

vegetarian: a person who eats a diet of foods derived from plants and who does not eat meat

Bibliography

Anderson, Margaret J. *Food Chains: The Unending Cycle*. Hillside, NJ: Enslow Publishers, 1991.

Angier, Natalie. *"In Recycling Waste, the Noble Scarab Is Peerless." New York Times*, December 10, 1991, C1.

Burnie, David. *How Nature Works*. Pleasantville, NY: Reader's Digest Association, 1991.

Current Science. "Colorful Frogs Get Their Poison from Their Dinner." November 28, 1997, 13.

Enger, Eldon D., and Frederick C. Ross. *Concepts in Biology*. 8th ed. Dubuque, IA: William C. Brown, 1997.

Hoagland, Mahlon, and Bert Dodson. *The Way Life Works*. New York: Times Books, 1995.

Levine, Joseph S., and Kenneth R. Miller. *Biology: Discovering Life*. 2nd ed. Lexington, MA: D. C. Heath and Company, 1994.

O'Toole, Christopher. *Alien Empire: An Exploration of the Lives of Insects*. New York: Harper Collins, 1995.

Pringle, Laurence. *Chains, Webs, and Pyramids: The Flow of Energy in Nature*. New York: Thomas Y. Crowell, 1975.

Smith, Robert Leo, and Thomas M. Smith. *Elements of Ecology*. 3rd ed. Boston, MA: Addison-Wesley, 1998.

Stevens, William K. "Search for Missing Otters Turns Up a Few Surprises." *New York Times*, January 5, 1999, F1–F2.

For Further Information

Books

Aloian, Molly, and Bobbie Kalman. *Rainforest Food Chains*. New York: Crabtree Publishing Company, 2006.

Capeci, Anne. *Food Chain Frenzy*. New York: Scholastic, 2004.

Kalman, Bobbie. *Coral Reef Food Chains*. New York: Crabtree Publishing Company, 2005.

———. *Food Chains and You*. New York: Crabtree Publishing Company, 2004.

Kalman, Bobbie, and Jacqueline Langille. *What Are Food Chains and Webs?* New York: Crabtree Publishing Company, 1998.

Revill, G. Alan. *Predators and Food Chains*. London: David Fulton Publishers, 2002.

Stewart, Melissa. *Life in a Wetland*, Ecosystems in Action series. Minneapolis: Twenty-First Century Books, 2003.

Wallace, Holly. *Food Chains and Webs*. Portsmouth, NH: Heinemann, 2006.

Web Sites

The Food Chain

http://library.advanced.org/11353/food.html. The site features definitions, role of humans, and also an audio discussion.

Food Chain

http://www.picadome.fcps.net/lab/currl/food_chain/default.html. This site has many links to information and fun activities, games, and movie clips about food chains and various ecosystems.

Food Chains: Prey and Predators

http://www.cas.psu.edu/docs/webcourse/wetland/wet1/main.html. This site has information and activities about typical wetland food chains and food webs.

Food Chains and Food Webs: What's for Dinner?

http://www.enchantedlearning.com/subjects/foodchain/. Information and activities about food chains and food webs are available on this site, with printable worksheets.

Science Online: Food Production and Energy for Life

http://classroom.jc-schools.net/sci-units/food.html. There are many links to information about plants, animals, food chains, and ecosystems on this site. It also includes activities.

Index

algae, 11, 27, 45, 53, 55, 62, 63
alkaloids, 32
alligators, 66
amino acids, 78–80
antelope, 20, 21, 29
ATP (adenosine
    triphosphate), 56
autotrophs, 12, 15

bacteria, 8, 11, 13, 15, 50, 51,
    74, 78, 83
balance of nature, 4–9, 26, 35,
    55, 76
ballast water, 70, 71
batrachotoxin, 32
bioconcentration, 63
biodiversity, 23, 24
biogeochemical cycles, 47, 48,
    59;
        carbon cycle, 53–56;
        nitrogen cycle, 50, 51;
        oxygen cycle, 52, 53;
        phosphorus cycle, 56–59;
        water cycle, 48
biological community, 6, 13,
    23–26, 28
biological magnification, 62, 63
biological pest control, 67, 68,
    70
biomass, 41, 42
birds, 29, 34, 38, 40, 41, 58,
    62, 64, 71; brown
    pelicans, 64; California
    condors, 64; eagles, 29,
    64; falcons, 29; goshawks,
    35; great horned owls, 35;
    ospreys, 62, 64; owls, 27,
    28; peregrine falcons, 43,
    63, 64; spotted owls, 27,
    28; vultures, 15, 16

bivalves, 31–33, 74
blue sac syndrome, 69
Borneo, 60
breastfeeding, 74

calories, 42
camouflage, 33
cane toads, 69
carbohydrates, 11
carbon cycle, 53–56
carbon dioxide, 9, 11, 12, 47,
    48, 52–56
carnivores, 15, 17, 18, 40, 79
cellulose, 78
cesium, 72
Chan, George, 81, 83, 84
cheetahs, 29
chemosynthesis, 13
chlorophyll, 11, 12
clams, 31, 32, 62, 71, 74
colon cancer, 78
complete proteins, 79, 80
compost heap, 17
consumers, 6–8, 13, 15, 41, 43,
    53, 55
cows, 14, 15, 72, 78
crabs, 13, 70, 71; green crabs,
    70, 71

DDT, 60–64, 69, 75
decomposers, 6–9, 15–19, 48,
    51, 57
deer, 4, 15, 26, 29
dicofol, 66
dioxins, 68, 69
DNA, 56
dung beetle, 19

ecological pyramids, 38–45, 62
ecology, defined, 6

ecosystem, 7, 16, 20, 25, 27, 28, 35, 39, 40, 44–48, 59, 60, 63, 69, 70, 81, 82
elephants, 24
Elton, Charles S., 38–41
energy flow in food chains, 10–19
Environmental Protection Agency (EPA), 69
essential amino acids, 79, 80
estrogens, 65
eucalyptus trees, 22
extinction, 64

fats, 44, 53, 77
Fiji, 81–83
fish, 26, 27, 29, 58, 62–66, 68, 69, 73–75, 77, 79, 81, 83
fish farming, 81, 82
fleas, 30, 45, 61
Florida Everglades, 67
Florida panthers, 65, 66
food chains, defined, 5, 6
food webs, 20, 21, 23, 25, 26, 45, 62, 69; keystone species, 25–27; population explosions, 35, 36; predators and prey, 5, 28–37, 76; umbrella species, 27, 28;
Forest Service, 5
fossil fuels, 54, 55
foxes, 8, 10, 15, 29, 38, 41, 42
frogs, 17, 28, 30, 32
fruit bats, 24
fungi, 8, 15, 57

giant panda, 22
glucose, 12, 37
glycogen, 37
grasshoppers, 15, 32
Great Lakes, 68, 69, 73
guano, 58

Haeckel, Ernst, 6
heart disease, 78
herbivores, 15, 17, 18, 78, 79
heterotrophs, 15
hormone pollutants, 64–66, 73, 75
human population, 76
hydrothermal vents, 13
hypertension, 78

insects, 18, 28, 32, 34, 35, 38, 40, 41, 60, 61; bees, 34; butterflies, 26, 34
integrated farming, 81–84
iodine, 72

Jacobson, Joseph, 74
Jacobson, Sandra, 74

Kaibab National Forest, Arizona, 4–6, 9, 26
kangaroos, 30
keystone species, 25–27
Klimley, A. Peter, 44
koalas, 22

lacto-ovo-vegetarians, 77
lacto-vegetarians, 77
Lake Apopka, 66
Lake Mead, Nevada, 65
Lake Michigan, 74
Lake Ontario, 75
lake trout, 68, 69
lions, 20, 21
lynxes, 35, 36

mad cow disease, 14
malaria, 60
meat, 41, 42, 76–79, 81
melaleuca, 67, 68
mice, 30, 41
mollusks, 74
mosquitoes, 26, 60

mountain lions, 4, 15, 25–27, 30
mule deer, 4, 5, 9, 26
mussels, 13, 75

National Cancer Institute, 72
Nevada Test Site, 72
niches, 7
nitrogen, 11, 50, 51, 54, 83
nitrogen cycle, 50, 51
nitrogen fixers, 50, 51
nuclear testing, 72
nutrient recycling, 46–59

obesity, 77
omnivores, 15, 17, 18, 79
ovo-vegetarians, 77
oxygen, 12, 52–54, 56
oxygen cycle, 52, 53
oystercatchers, 31, 32
oysters, 31, 32, 71, 74

pesco-vegetarians, 77
pesticides, 60, 64, 66, 67
phosphates, 56, 57
phosphorus cycle, 56–59
photosynthesis, 11–13, 16, 47, 52, 53, 55, 56
phytoplankton, 58
plants, 4–6, 8, 9, 11, 12, 14–17, 20, 23, 24, 26, 36, 38, 41, 43, 47–57, 62, 67, 71, 76, 78, 79
poison, 32, 52, 60, 61, 68, 69, 73
pollution, 25, 64, 65, 67, 73–75, 81, 82
polychlorinated biphenyls (PCBs), 68, 69, 73–75
population explosions, 35, 36
predators, 28–32, 34–37, 45, 69

pregnancy, 74
prey animals, 28–30, 32, 36, 37, 45, 58
primary consumers, 14, 17, 18, 28, 38, 39, 45, 62
primary producers, 17, 18, 62
producers, 6–8, 12, 17, 18, 38, 39, 43, 45, 55, 56
proteins, 50, 53, 65, 79, 80
pyramid of biomass, 41, 42, 45
pyramid of energy, 42, 43, 45
pyramid of numbers, 39, 40, 45

quaternary consumers, 17, 18

rabbits, 8, 10, 15, 29, 30, 35, 36, 41, 42
raccoons, 15, 66
radiation, 72
radioisotopes, 72
rads, 72
rainwater, 49, 56, 57
recycling, 17, 46, 47, 50–52, 56, 57, 59
respiration, 53, 55
River Lee, England, 65
RNA, 56

saturated fat, 77
scallops, 31
scavengers, 15–18, 41, 42
sea lamprey, 68
sea otters, 32–44
sea stars, 31
secondary consumers, 17, 18, 28, 38, 39, 62
semi-vegetarians, 77
sex hormones, 65
sharks, 26, 27, 29, 44
shellfish, 31, 71, 74
skunks, 34, 35

snout beetles, 68, 69
snowshoe rabbits, 35–37
soybean products, 80
sperm counts, 75
spiders, 33
starches, 11
strontium, 72
sugars, 11, 12, 37, 52, 53, 79
sunlight, 10–13, 18, 24, 53

teeth, human, 79
"10 percent rule," 44, 45
tertiary consumers, 17, 18, 38, 39, 62
thyroid cancer, 72
trophic levels, 16–18, 23, 38, 39, 41, 42, 44–46, 63, 73
tube worms, 13
turtles, 20, 30, 31

umbrella species, 27, 28
United Nations Economic Commission for Europe, 75
U.S. Geological Survey, 65

vegans, 77, 78
vegetarians, 77, 78, 80, 81
vitellogenin, 65
volcanoes, 13, 56

water, 11, 12, 22, 46–53, 55, 57, 58, 63, 65, 74, 83
water cycle, 48, 50
water pollution, 64–66, 68–69, 73–75
whales, 29, 44
World Health Organization, 60

zebras, 20, 21

Photo Acknowledgments

The images in this book are used with the permission of: Animals Animals (© Mickey Gibson, p. 5; © Ralph Reinhold, p. 43 (top); © James Robinson, p. 66); © Laura Westlund/Independent Picture Service, pp. 6, 12, 49, 52; Visuals Unlimited (© Ron Spomer, p. 7; © Joe McDonald, pp. 8, 25, 29; © Gerry Bishop, p. 9; © Dr. Joe Henderson, p. 11; © Masa Ushioda, p. 27; © Rob & Ann Simpson, p. 30; © Francis/Donna Caldwell, p. 31; © Bill Beatty, pp. 33, 48; © Charles Melton, p. 34; © William Ormerod, p. 43 (second from bottom); © David Sieren, p. 43 (bottom); © David Wrobel, p. 58; © Ken Wagner, p. 67; © David B. Fleetham, p. 83); © Jaime Reina/ AFP/Getty Images, p. 16; © Ron Miller, pp. 18, 23, 39, 51, 55, 57, 62; © Mitsuaki Iwago/Minden Pictures, p. 21 (top); © James Warwick/The Image Bank/Getty Images, p. 21 (bottom); © Greg Vaughn/Stone/Getty Images, p. 28; © Tom & Pat Leeson, p. 36; © Laurance B. Aiuppy/Taxi/ Getty Images, p. 40; © age fotostock/ SuperStock, pp. 41, 43 (second from top), 82; © Justin Sullivan/Getty Images, p. 47; © China Photos/Getty Images, p. 54; Agricultural Research Service, USDA, p. 61; © Galen Rowell/ CORBIS, p. 63; © BIOS Gunther Michel/Peter Arnold, Inc., p. 70; © Getty Images, p. 73; USDA Photo, p. 76; © James Meyer/The Image Bank/Getty Images, p. 80. Front cover: © Jeremy Woodhouse/ Photographer's Choice/Getty Images.

About the Authors

Dr. Alvin Silverstein is a former professor of biology and director of the Physician Assistant Program at the College of Staten Island of the City University of New York. Virginia B. Silverstein is a translator of Russian scientific literature.

The Silversteins' collaboration began with a biochemical research project at the University of Pennsylvania. Since then they have produced six children and more than two hundred published books that have received high acclaim for their clear, timely, and authoritative coverage of science and health topics.

Laura Silverstein Nunn, a graduate of Kean College, began helping with the research for her parents' books while she was in high school. Since joining the writing team, she has coauthored more than eighty books.